The
Barbara Pym
Cookbook

The
Barbara Pym
Cookbook

HILARY PYM & HONOR WYATT

OPEN ROAD

INTEGRATED MEDIA

NEW YORK

CONTENTS

MAIN DISHES 15

LUNCH AND SUPPER DISHES   41

"TRIED FAVOURITES"   93

INTRODUCTORY NOTE

This book may not come as a surprise to readers of my sister's novels, who often comment on her many references to eating and food: carefully prepared meals (successful or unsuccessful), restaurant lunches, gourmet dishes, solitary suppers (actual or in prospect), Sunday family dinners, packed lunches and party food, teas of all kinds, breakfasts large and small—so that the question arises, Was she herself a good cook? Did she eat as well as some of her characters? I admit I never saw her prepare Sole Nantua, so memorable for Adam Prince in *A Few Green Leaves*, but I do remember an afternoon spent making ravioli (which Belinda in *Some Tame Gazelle* chose to make when she had the kitchen to herself), and the long, slow cooking of a cassoulet, of duck I think, when she decided that a tin of baked beans might have had exactly the same result. She enjoyed cooking in a creative way and liked to write down the menus we had when people came to eat with us, so I have been able to refer to these in compiling this book. I have also asked Honor Wyatt to collaborate with me in making the recipes, because as well as being a professional writer on the subject (I think her *Crisis Cookery* could still find a place in many households), she must have had an influence on Barbara's interest in cooking when we were sharing a house together in Bristol during the 1940s. The result is a combination, I hope, of practical—perhaps overfamiliar, for which I apologize—recipes for cooks, and useful references or reminders for Pym readers who are more interested in the idea and the associations of food than the actual preparation of it. But, as Wilf Bason says, what poetry there is in cooking!

—HILARY PYM

A NOTE ON THE RECIPES

There are equivalents and there are equivalents. In this book the equivalents between ounces and milliliters, pounds and grams, will work in your kitchen, not in the lab. Where precise amounts are important, as with baking, we have made every effort possible to ensure your success. The amounts of some ingredients or length of cooking time may vary according to altitude, oven temperature calibration, moisture content of flour, and the like. However, all of these recipes can be managed fairly easily.

In the British kitchen, tablespoons and teaspoons sometimes refer to somewhat larger utensils than are used in the United States. Standard measuring spoon measures are used in these recipes. So, a teaspoon has nothing to do with the item to the right of your dinner plate, but refers to the specific kitchen utensil so designated. You will run across a dessertspoon measure in some of the more traditional recipes. This standard British measure translates to 4 level teaspoons.

Liquid is sometimes measured in glass sizes and teacups in the British kitchen. As a guide, you can figure a teacup to be somewhat less than a cup, or about ¾ cup (225 ml). A wine glass measure also equals about ¾ cup (225 ml). A brandy glass of spirits measures roughly 2–3 tablespoons.

When baking you may be called upon to bake a pie shell "blind," or prebake it. To do this, prepare your pastry, roll it out, line the pie tin, crimp the edges, and chill. To bake it blind, line the shell with foil or greaseproof paper, weight it with raw rice, beans, or pie weights, and bake at 400°F (200°C) for 10 minutes. Remove the weights and foil, prick the bottom of the shell with the tines of a fork, then return to the oven and bake for an additional 5 minutes to brown lightly. Set aside to cool, then proceed with your recipe.

Mixed spice, when called for, can include a selection of your favourite seasonings. A blend sometimes referred to as Spice Parisienne is recommended. Combine 1 tablespoon of cinnamon with 1 teaspoon each of ground cloves, ground ginger, and ground nutmeg. Use as needed.

Mixed herbs are even more a matter of taste. You can purchase one of the many mixtures commonly available at the market, or you can make up your own blend. A good basic mixture includes basil, thyme, oregano or marjoram, and savory. You are encouraged to experiment—add other herbs, adjust quantities—according to your own preferences.

Several recipes call for cheese. In these cases, use a good cheddar, Gruyère, or Parmesan.

Starters
and Soups

"Ah!" said George, as prawn cocktail was placed before us and white wine poured into one of the two glasses that stood at every place, and he began to eat purposefully.

—AN ACADEMIC QUESTION

Prawn cocktails, smoked salmon, potted shrimps need no recipes here. But the first course might be a mousse.

SALMON OR TUNA MOUSSE

½ ounce (15 g) gelatin, softened in ¼ cup (75 ml) cold water

8-ounce (225 g) tin salmon or tuna or fresh salmon, cooked

½ cup (150 ml) light cream or evaporated milk

1 teaspoon lemon juice

2 tablespoons mayonnaise

1 cucumber, peeled and grated or chopped

Salt and pepper to taste

Stir in ¾ cup (225 ml) boiling water to softened gelatin and set aside. In a small bowl, flake fish with a fork, discarding skin, and set aside. Whip cream or milk until thick, then blend in lemon juice and mayonnaise. Add gelatin mixture, fish, and cucumber. Season well and mix thoroughly. Turn into an oiled 1-pint (600 ml) mold or small individual dishes. Chill about 4 hours until firm. Emma Howick in *A Few Green Leaves* decorated her tuna mousse with sliced cucumber "of exquisite thinness."

"It is an art all too seldom met with," Adam declared, "the correct slicing of cucumber. In Victorian times there was—I believe—an implement or device for the purpose."

—A FEW GREEN LEAVES

Emma had probably used the same recipe some months earlier for her ham mousse, which she had turned out on the same flowered dish.

With less effort than that required for the mousse, Emma could have made her ham into this simple version of the old-fashioned potted meat.

POTTED HAM

8 ounces (225 g) cooked ham, minced

Freshly ground black pepper to taste

Powdered mace to taste

Chopped parsley to taste

8 tablespoons clarified butter

Pound or mash together the ham, seasonings, and parsley. Pack tightly into little jars. Pour clarified butter over, cover, and refrigerate until ready to use. Serve with toast or rolls.

Rollo Gaunt, in *An Academic Question*, recalled "a memorable asparagus mousse" eaten "in that delightful French restaurant, chez something or other."

ASPARAGUS MOUSSE

8 ounces (225 g) fresh green asparagus, trimmed

1 ounce (30 g) gelatin, softened in ¼ cup (75 ml) cold water, then added to
¼ cup (75 ml) hot chicken or vegetable stock

½ cup (150 ml) mayonnaise

½ cup (150 ml) double or heavy cream

Juice of ½ lemon

Salt and pepper to taste

Cook the asparagus gently in boiling salted water until tender, then purée it, reserving some of the tips for garnishing. Combine puréed asparagus with remaining ingredients and blend or whisk together. Place reserved asparagus tips decoratively in an oiled mold or individual dishes, spoon mousse over, cover, and refrigerate about 4 hours until set.

23 April. Philip Larkin to lunch. We had sherry and then the wine (burgundy) Bob gave me for Christmas (was this rather insensitive to Bob?). We ate kipper pâté, then veal done with peppers and tomatoes, pommes Anna and celery & cheese (he didn't eat any Brie and we thought perhaps he only likes plain food). He's shy but very responsive and jokey. Hilary took our photo together and he left about 3:30 in his large Rover car (pale tobacco brown).

—A VERY PRIVATE EYE

KIPPER PÂTÉ

8-ounce (225 g) pack kipper fillets or smoked mackerel

3 tablespoons wine vinegar

8 tablespoons butter or margarine, softened

2 ounces (60 g) cream cheese, softened

Freshly ground black pepper to taste

Place kippers or mackerel in a shallow dish, add boiling water, and let sit for a few minutes. Drain, skin fish, then return fillets to shallow dish. Add wine vinegar, cover, and refrigerate overnight. Pound or mash fillets with butter, cream cheese, and pepper. Chill before serving.

"In Greece cucumber is cut in chunks, thick chunks," said Daphne. "It makes a lovely salad, with tomatoes and *plenty* of oil." She cast about in her memory for the Greek word for this particular salad, failed to remember it, but then decided that nobody would have been interested anyway.

"Greek food is not one of my favourites," said Adam, smiling. "One would hardly go to Greece for the cuisine—just as one wouldn't go to some churches for the music. A beautiful country, of course," he smiled again as if at some private joke, "but not a treasury of gastronomic memories."

—A FEW GREEN LEAVES

With her passionate interest in Greece, Daphne might have preferred the first course to be *dolmadhes*. These should be made with vine leaves—when Barbara and I lived in Brooksville Avenue in London N.W. 6, we had a vine growing up against the house so we occasionally made them—but cabbage leaves make a good substitute.

DOLMADHES

2 small onions

¾ pound (350 g) finely ground beef

Salt and pepper to taste

3 tablespoons cooked rice

1 small head of cabbage

Beef stock

1 bay leaf

Thin tomato sauce

Preheat oven to 350°F (180°C). Chop onions very finely, put in a bowl with meat and seasonings, mix together, and add water (about 7 tablespoons) gradually, until well blended. Add rice and set aside. Put whole cabbage into boiling water and cook 2 to 3 minutes. Drain well and detach leaves, cutting away and discarding any hard bits of stalk. Put a small tablespoon of meat mixture on each leaf and roll up into a sausage-shaped parcel, turning in the edges. Arrange parcels in criss-crossed layers in a stewpan or casserole, making sure the seam sides are down. Add enough stock to cover, bring to a boil, add bay leaf, reduce heat, cover, and simmer 20 minutes. Transfer the *dolmadhes* to an ovenproof dish, discarding the stock and bay leaf. Over them, pour enough tomato sauce to cover, cover the dish, and bake about 30 minutes.

Daphne would no doubt also have experienced the yogurt and cucumber dish called *tsatsiki* by the Greeks.

TSATSIKI

1 pint (600 ml) plain yogurt

1 cucumber, peeled and diced

3 cloves garlic, minced

Coarsely chopped mint leaves to taste

Salt and pepper to taste

Paprika for garnish (optional)

Mix all ingredients together, cover, and refrigerate. Serve very cold, garnished with paprika, if desired.

An alternative could be stuffed tomatoes or tomatoes à la Provençale, but Dulcie Mainwaring in *No Fond Return of Love* would have decided against these when she was entertaining Aylwin Forbes:

Viola had . . . remarked that Aylwin had once said he didn't like tomatoes. Dulcie, therefore, had been careful to avoid any dish containing these "love apples," as she now called them to herself, saying over the phrase "Aylwin can't take love apples" with a good deal of enjoyment.

——NO FOND RETURN OF LOVE

TOMATOES À LA PROVENÇALE

Choose large ripe tomatoes and cut them in half. Hollow them out a little, and stuff them with a mixture of the removed flesh combined with bread crumbs, chopped garlic, and parsley, moistened with olive oil. Cook under the grill or in a hot oven until well-browned.

LASTLY, SOUPS.

"I thought perhaps a cold meal, but I've made one of *my* soups," Leonora was saying, "just for your first evening back. Then Humphrey wants us to go round for coffee and drinks. But first let me show you your *own* little kitchen. . . ."
—THE SWEET DOVE DIED

CONSOMMÉ MOUSSE

10½-ounce (298 g) tin beef consommé (undiluted)

8 ounces (225 g) cream cheese

Curry powder to taste

Chopped chives or parsley for garnish (optional)

Have all ingredients at room temperature. Whisk together consommé and cream cheese until well blended, then stir in curry powder. Pour into small dishes, cover, and chill for several hours. Serve garnished with chopped chives or parsley, if you wish.

A variation on vegetable soups was given to us by Elizabeth Harvey, the sister of Henry Harvey who became Archdeacon Hoccleve in *Some Tame Gazelle*, Barbara's first novel and the only one whose "characters were taken directly from life" as she tells us in *A Very Private Eye*.

CARROT SOUP WITH ORANGE

1 pound (450 g) carrots, chopped

1 onion, chopped

1 clove garlic, minced

4 tablespoons oil or melted butter

4 cups (1 l) chicken or vegetable stock

Salt and pepper to taste

Juice of 2 oranges

Grated rind of 1 orange

1 teaspoon brown sugar

Cook the carrots, onion, and garlic in oil or butter until softened, about 10 minutes. Add the stock, season, and simmer until tender. Purée in a blender or put through a sieve. Add the orange juice and grated rind, and return to stove. Reheat, add sugar, taste, and adjust seasoning. Serve quite hot.

The third soup is a Greek one. Barbara and I were among the first people who went to Greece by coach from London—starting from Marylebone Station on a Thursday evening and arriving in Athens on Monday night—in 1966. A dish of this egg-and-lemon soup at a restaurant just over the frontier was very comforting, even in hot weather.

AVGOLEMONO SOUP

4 cups (1 l) chicken stock

2 ounces (60 g) rice or vermicelli

2 eggs

Juice of 1 large lemon

Boil the rice or vermicelli in the chicken stock until cooked. In a small bowl, beat together the eggs and lemon juice. Gradually add some of the hot stock, stirring constantly until thickened. Stir egg-stock mixture into the rest of the stock and reheat, but do not let it boil.

Main Dishes

"Tom, the bay leaf I'm putting in this *boeuf à la mode* was plucked from a tree growing in the garden of Thomas Hardy's birthplace," Catherine called from the kitchen. She did not really expect an answer and indeed none came from Tom, sitting hunched over his typewriter, so she went on, almost to herself, "I wonder if it's *wrong* of me to use it for cooking? Perhaps I ought to have pressed it in *Jude the Obscure*, or the poems, that would have been more suitable."

. . . Oh, what joy to get a real calf's foot from the butcher, she thought, and not to have to cheat by putting in gelatine. The small things of life were often so much bigger than the great things, she decided, wondering how many writers and philosophers had said this before her, the trivial pleasures like cooking, one's home, little poems especially sad ones, solitary walks, funny things seen and overheard.

—LESS THAN ANGELS

BOEUF À LA MODE

2 pounds (900 g) beef topside or top round

Bacon fat or drippings

Salt and pepper to taste

2 onions, sliced

1 small bunch of carrots, sliced

1 head of celery, trimmed and sliced

Bouquet garni (thyme, bay leaf, whole peppercorns, whole cloves, grated orange or lemon peel, tied in a cheesecloth bag)

1 calf's foot

Beef stock or water

Red wine

Brown the meat on all sides in bacon fat or drippings. Season and put in a casserole with sliced vegetables, bouquet garni, and calf's foot. Pour in equal parts stock or water and wine to cover. Cook over very low heat, covered, for 2 to 3 hours. Remove meat, which should be so soft it can be cut with a spoon, and put it on a serving dish. Strain the sauce over, discarding solids, and let cool. When cooled, remove fat. Meat should be covered with a clear jelly. Slice beef and cube calf's foot, and serve them together.

The bay tree that now grows in my front garden in Finstock came from a cutting that Barbara took, not from Hardy's birthplace, but from the garden in Henley that belonged to her friends John and Elizabeth Barnicot. (John Barnicot became the character John Akenside in *Some Tame Gazelle*.) A bay leaf was an important ingredient of another beef dish that the young clergyman Basil Branche in *An Unsuitable Attachment* would have appreciated:

"Imparadised in one another's arms," as Milton put it, Basil went on. "Or encasseroled, perhaps—the bay leaf resting on the *boeuf bourguignon*."

BOEUF BOURGUIGNON

1 pound (450 g) braising or stewing beef, cut in cubes

1 onion, sliced

1 carrot, diced

1 bay leaf

Thyme and whole peppercorns to taste

2 tablespoons oil

2 glasses red wine

Flour

Butter or margarine

½ pound (225 g) button mushrooms

4 ounces (110 g) bacon, diced

12 small onions, peeled

Marinate meat, onion slices, carrot, and herbs for 24 hours in oil and wine. Strain marinade and reserve it, discarding solids. Pat meat dry, roll cubes in flour, and sauté in butter or margarine until browned. Place meat in a stewpan. Sauté mushrooms, bacon, and whole onions in butter, then add to beef. Pour reserved marinade over all, cover, and simmer 1½ to 2 hours.

Roast beef might have been the more conventional choice of Belinda Bede in *Some Tame Gazelle,* as she and Harriet planned the dinner party to which Archdeacon Hoccleve and Mr. Donne were to be invited.

The day had begun as other Sundays did. After breakfast Belinda had consulted with Emily about the roast beef, and together they had decided what time it ought to be put into the oven and how long it ought to stay there. The vegetables—celery and roast potatoes—were agreed upon, and the pudding—a plum tart—chosen. In addition, the chickens for the supper party were to be put on to boil and Emily was to start making the trifle if she had time. The jellies had been made on Saturday night and were now setting in the cool of the cellar. Belinda had suggested that they might have a lighter luncheon than usual, as there was so much to do, but Harriet was not going to be cheated of her Sunday roast, and had managed to persuade her sister that there would be plenty of time to get things ready in the afternoon and early evening. It was of course out of the question that either of them should attend Evensong.

When curates came to supper the traditional choice was a boiled chicken:

Were all new curates everywhere always given boiled chicken when they came to supper for the first time? Belinda wondered. It was certainly an established ritual at their house and it seemed somehow right for a new curate. The coldness, the whiteness, the muffling with sauce, perhaps even the sharpness added by the slices of lemon, there was something appropriate here, even if Belinda could not see exactly what it was.

——SOME TAME GAZELLE

A "boiling fowl" has now become a thing of the past, and I don't think Barbara boiled many chickens in later years. She would roast them, of course, but not in such quantities as did Everard Bone's mother in *Excellent Women:*

"Read this." She handed me a cutting headed OWL BITES WOMAN, from which I read that an owl had flown in through a cottage window one evening and bitten a woman on the chin. "And this," she went on, handing me another cutting which told how a swan had knocked a girl off her bicycle. "What do you think of *that?*"

"The Dominion of the Birds," she went on. "I very much fear it may come to that."

Everard looked at me a little anxiously but I managed to keep up the conversation until Mrs. Bone declared that it was dinner time.

"I eat as many birds as possible," said Mrs. Bone when we were sitting down to roast chicken. "I have them sent from Harrods or Fortnum's, and sometimes I go and look at them in the cold meats department. They do them up very prettily with aspic jelly and decorations. At least we can eat our enemies."

——EXCELLENT WOMEN

Or she might choose to have chicken with tarragon, as Leonora did for James in *The Sweet Dove Died.* No doubt Leonora would have given it its French name, *poulet sauté à l'estragon.*

CHICKEN WITH TARRAGON

1 chicken, cut into 8 pieces

3 tablespoons butter or oil

1 small onion, chopped

1 tablespoon flour

1 glass white wine

½ cup (150 ml) chicken stock

Finely chopped tarragon leaves to taste

Salt and pepper to taste

Sauté chicken pieces in butter or oil until lightly browned. Remove to a platter and keep warm. In the same pan, sauté chopped onion, stir in flour, and cook 2 to 3 minutes. Add wine, stock, tarragon, and seasonings. Cook to reduce somewhat. Return chicken pieces to pan, cover, and simmer in sauce 20 minutes. To serve, place chicken pieces on a platter and pour sauce over.

This dish was named after our cat, who liked tomato skins.

POULET MINERVA

½ teaspoon ground cinnamon

½ teaspoon ground cloves

Juice of 1 lemon

Salt and pepper to taste

1 chicken, cut in pieces

¼ cup (75 ml) oil

4 tablespoons butter

6 tomatoes, peeled and chopped

2 tablespoons tomato purée

Combine cinnamon, cloves, lemon juice, salt, and pepper, and rub mixture onto chicken. Heat oil and butter in a frying pan and brown chicken pieces. Remove chicken to a platter and keep warm. Add tomatoes and tomato purée to frying pan and stir in about 1 pint (600 ml) water. Cook over a gentle heat until the tomatoes are soft, then add chicken pieces and cook until tender, about 20 to 25 minutes.

"This is one of Father Lydell's favourite dishes," said Beth, bringing a covered casserole to the table. *Poulet niçoise*—I hope you like it."

"Oh, yes," Letty murmured, remembering the times she had eaten *poulet niçoise* at Marjorie's house. Had David Lydell gone all round the village sampling the cooking of the unattached women before deciding which one to settle with? Certainly the dish they were eating this evening was well up to standard.

—QUARTET IN AUTUMN

POULET NIÇOISE

1 chicken, cut in pieces

4 tablespoons butter

¼ cup (75 ml) oil

½ cup (150 ml) white wine

1 teaspoon saffron

4 cloves garlic, crushed with 1 teaspoon salt

Bouquet garni (1 sprig each of thyme and rosemary, and 1 or 2 bay leaves, tied in a cheesecloth bag)

Tin of tomatoes, about 2 cups (600 ml)

Salt and pepper to taste

8 to 10 black olives

Sauté chicken pieces in butter and oil until browned. Transfer to a fireproof casserole, add wine and ½ cup (150 ml) water. To the sauté pan, add saffron, garlic with salt, bouquet garni, and tomatoes. Season, and simmer until tomatoes are soft. Pour over chicken, add olives, cover, and cook very gently for 1 to 1½ hours

I don't remember that we ever had chicken *forestière*:

"Vegetables and that," said Norman. "I suppose that's what *forestière* means—things from the forest. Though you wouldn't really get vegetables in a forest, would you?"

"This has mushrooms in it," said Letty, "and you might certainly find those in a wood or forest."

"But you wouldn't fancy them," said Norman, "not out of the forest."

—QUARTET IN AUTUMN

Duck isn't always as successful as chicken. When Archdeacon Hoccleve preached his famous Judgment Day sermon in *Some Tame Gazelle* and delayed everybody's Sunday lunch, Belinda knew that they were having duck at the vicarage: " 'And of course,' she said thoughtfully, as she watched her sister carve the overcooked beef, 'duck needs to be *very* well done, doesn't it? It can't really be cooked too much.' " *(Some Tame Gazelle)*

DUCK WITH OLIVES

1 large duck, giblets reserved

Salt and freshly ground black pepper to taste

Flour

Green olives, sliced

Preheat oven to 450°F (230°C). Pat duck with towel to dry well, then prick skin all over with a sharp fork, and rub skin with salt and pepper. Put duck in a roasting pan, preferably on a rack, adding no fat at all. Roast 30 minutes, then turn down heat to 350°F (180°C) and roast for at least 2 hours more, pouring off fat occasionally. Boil the duck giblets with water to make some stock. Remove duck to a serving platter and keep warm. Add some flour to the juices in the roasting pan and cook over low heat for about 3 minutes. Blend in stock to make a gravy. Add sliced green olives and serve gravy with duck.

"How convenient women were," Rupert Stonebird thought, in *An Unsuitable Attachment*, "the way they were always 'just going' to make coffee or tea, or perhaps had just roasted a joint in the oven or made a cheese soufflé."

Dulcie Mainwaring in *No Fond Return of Love* had roasted her joint of lamb to perfection in a slow oven and made it fragrant with sprigs of rosemary. Here is another recipe for roast lamb, which Barbara often used.

ROAST DIJON LAMB

Preheat oven to 450°F (230°C). Spread a lamb joint, leg or shoulder, with Dijon mustard, and sprinkle all over with chopped thyme and minced garlic. Set roast on a rack and place uncovered in oven. Lower heat to 350°F (180°C) and cook until desired doneness, about 30 minutes per pound for well-done.

I have already referred to a casserole being brought to the table. Emma Howick in *A Few Green Leaves* thought she might be expected to carry one through the woods to Graham Pettifer's cottage if she was to cook occasionally for him:

"I thought I'd see if you'd settled in all right, got your milk and the groceries from the shop." Did I once love this man? Emma asked herself, feeling that perhaps they should have kissed or at least greeted each other a little more warmly.

"Yes, thank you—the milk came this morning and I found the box of groceries—rather an odd selection."

"Odd? In what way? I just asked them to put in some necessities, bread and butter and cheese and various tins, to tide you over."

Graham smiled. "I just thought it seemed odd to have tinned vegetables in the country—I'd imagined produce from people's gardens, even yours. And I don't *much* care for spaghetti hoops."

"I don't grow vegetables," said Emma, feeling nettled (surely that was the appropriate word?). "You'll probably be glad of a tin of peas or carrots one of these days. As for the spaghetti hoops, I suppose Mrs. Bland at the shop thought they'd do for a light supper dish."

"We obviously have different ideas about supper. Oh, and there was a loaf of *sliced* bread. . . . I was hoping you'd come last night—bring something you'd cooked yourself. I've got a good collection of suitable wines inside."

He might have hoped for pork chops or fillet.

PORK CHOPS WITH APPLE

4 pork chops

Oil or butler

1 onion, chopped

1 tart cooking apple, peeled, cored, and sliced

1 cup (300 ml) cider

Salt and pepper to taste

½ cup (150 ml) light cream

Preheat oven to 350°F (180°C). In a sauté pan, brown pork chops in oil or butter, add onion, and cook until soft. Transfer chops and onion to a casserole, add apple slices, cider, and seasonings. Cover and bake about 45 minutes. Stir in cream before serving.

PORK OR VEAL FILLET
WITH PEPPERS AND TOMATOES

1 pound (450 g) pork or veal fillet (boneless tenderloin, rolled and tied)

Seasoned flour

Oil or butter

1 onion, sliced

1 green pepper, seeded and chopped

Tin of tomatoes, about 2 cups (600 ml)

1 tablespoon Worcestershire sauce

Juice of 1 lemon

1 dessertspoon sugar

½ cup (150 ml) pork or beef stock

Salt and pepper to taste

Preheat oven to 350°F (180°C). Dip meat in seasoned flour, and brown it in oil or butter. Transfer meat to a casserole. Add onion and green pepper to remaining oil or butter in pan and cook about 5 minutes. Add tomatoes, Worcestershire sauce, lemon juice, sugar, stock, and seasonings. Bring to a boil, then pour over meat in casserole. Cover and bake 1 hour, basting meat occasionally.

Sometime before the guests were due to arrive, Mark went down to the cellar to bring up the wine. He peered in the half darkness at the metal rack in which two bottles, the remains of an Easter present from Sophia's mother, sat in lonely dignity for each was a good wine of its kind.

"Red or white, darling?" he called, seeing that there was one of each.

"Red, I think," said Sophia. "It's a sort of casserole or beef stew we're having."

Mark picked up the dark-looking bottle to read the label.

"This seems to be port," he said, "so it will have to be the white. Oh, but *this* is the Niersteiner, the last bottle, and it wouldn't go very well with beef." He had been saving it for Sophia's birthday.

"Well, let them drink beer or cider," said Sophia. "Neither Edwin nor Daisy drinks much and I don't suppose Ianthe Broome does."

"So it's only Mr. Stonebird we're considering—as a clergyman's son and an anthropologist he might drink a great deal."

—AN UNSUITABLE ATTACHMENT

Sophia's dish could have been this one.

BEEF CASSEROLE WITH LENTILS

2 pounds (900 g) stewing beef, cut in cubes

2 tablespoons oil or rendered fat

2 onions, sliced

2 carrots, chopped or sliced

15 ounces (575 ml) beef stock

1 bay leaf

Salt and pepper to taste

4 ounces (110 g) brown lentils, soaked according to package directions and drained

Preheat oven to 275°F (140°C). Brown meat in oil or fat, and remove to a casserole. Fry the onions in remaining fat, add them with the carrots to beef in casserole, pour stock over, and add bay leaf and seasonings. Bake, covered, about 3 hours. Halfway through cooking, stir in lentils.

Rupert Stonebird was to have a more unusual dining experience:

"Do you like your house?" Penelope asked. "Are you happy in it?"

"Yes—and I have good neighbours which is pleasant . . . Do you know, one of them brought me an oxtail the other evening?"

"An *oxtail*?" Penelope saw it being carried in the hand, stiff and furry at one end like a kind of African fly switch. "Whatever for?"

"To eat—it was in a basin."

"Oh I see—cooked. But surely not a whole oxtail?"

"Well, I don't know—it lasted me two meals."

—AN UNSUITABLE ATTACHMENT

OXTAIL

1 oxtail, cut into serving pieces

Oil or drippings

2 onions, sliced

Tin of tomatoes, about 2 cups (600 ml)

1 teaspoon mixed herbs

Chopped garlic to taste

Salt and pepper to taste

Preheat oven to 325°F (160°C). In a sauté pan, brown oxtail pieces in oil or drippings, then remove to a casserole. Cook onions, tomatoes, herbs, garlic, and seasonings in pan until the onions are softened, then add to meat in casserole. Bake, covered, about 3 hours. Serve with rice.

The Italian Conte, Leonora's old friend with whom she was to dine in *The Sweet Dove Died*, liked to eat steak and kidney pudding and drink Guinness whenever he was in London (he was based on a real-life character)—and what could be more satisfying and more traditionally English? This is Honor's recipe.

STEAK AND KIDNEY PUDDING

4 ounces (110 g) shredded suet

1⅓ cups (225 g) self-raising flour

1 pound (450 g) rump steak, cut in 1-inch cubes

¼ pound (110 g) kidneys, each cut into 8 pieces

Flour seasoned with salt and pepper

1 teaspoon mixed herbs

Rub suet into flour until well combined, then add 1 tablespoon cold water at a time to make a soft dough. Cut off about two-thirds of the dough and roll out to about 1 inch thick, dust with flour, and fold in half. Pull the ends of the folded dough away from you to shape it into a bag. With dough, line a well-greased ovenproof basin or bowl, overlapping the top edges. Roll the meat pieces in seasoned flour and arrange in layers in lined basin, sprinkling herbs between layers. Add cold water until basin is three-fourths full. Roll out the remaining dough and cover top, overlapping edge, pressing both pieces of dough together securely to prevent steam from escaping. Trim edges. Tie a floured cloth over pudding and steam for 4 hours.

Turning now to fish, Adam Prince, the good-food inspector in *A Few Green Leaves*, actually gives the recipe for his memorable Sole Nantua:

"Sole Nantua," said Isobel . . . "That's a sauce, is it?"

"Yes, made with crayfish," Adam explained. "You would poach about a dozen small crayfish in a court bouillon with white wine and herbs."

——A FEW GREEN LEAVES

But Dulcie's memory, in *No Fond Return of Love*, doesn't serve her quite as well:

"It must be strange to live at the seaside all the year round," Viola observed. "Look—there's the hotel I was thinking of—the Bristol. It seems to be the biggest one. Shall we go in?"

"Yes, but let's peer first," said Dulcie. "This is the dining-room, obviously."

A middle-aged couple, looking like people in an advertisement—she in pearls and a silver fox cape over a black dress, he in a dark suit—sat at a table in the window. A waiter bent over them—"deferentially," Dulcie supposed, helping them to some fish—turbot, surely? Its white flesh was exposed before them. How near to the heart of things it seemed!

"What is that sauce one has with turbot?" Dulcie asked. "*Du* something or other. I suppose this is only one course of dinner at the Hotel Bristol. I feel quite hungry again."

So here it is.

TURBOT, HALIBUT, OR SOLE DUGLÉRÉ

2 or 3 tomatoes, skinned

2 tablespoons butter

2 dessertspoons flour

1 cup (300 ml) fish stock or fish cooking liquid

2 dessertspoons chopped parsley

¼ cup (75 ml) double or heavy cream

Cooked turbot, halibut, or sole

Remove pulp from tomatoes and rub through a sieve. Reserve. Cut tomatoes into strips and set aside. Melt butter, stir in flour, and cook 2 to 3 minutes. Blend in sieved tomato pulp and fish stock, bring to a simmer, and cook 3 to 5 minutes. Add tomato strips and parsley, heat, then stir in cream but do not boil. Flake the fish, mix with the sauce, and serve in small dishes.

Before Mr. Bason's installation, Wilmet Forsyth in *A Glass of Blessings* imagines the scene at the clergy house:

A sudden anxious picture came into my mind—the two priests in the clergy house kitchen, trying to cook fillets of plaice or cod steaks. Perhaps in the end they would have to open a tin of sardines or spaghetti, unless they had decided to dine out. They might even have got a housekeeper by now. How wonderful it would be if Father Thames had interviewed and engaged Mr. Bason, and he was even now preparing them a delicious sole Véronique! I saw him at the kitchen table, peeling grapes. Of course I had no idea what he looked like—I just saw his fingers, long and sensitive as befitted an Anglo-Catholic fond of cooking, removing the pips.

SOLE VÉRONIQUE

2 tablespoons bread crumbs

1 tablespoon shredded suet

1 dessertspoon chopped parsley

1 egg, lightly beaten

Salt and pepper to taste

Pinch of mixed herbs

3 small fillets of sole

Peeled grapes, for garnish

Make a forcemeat stuffing of the first six ingredients, using as much of the beaten egg as necessary to bind all together. Spread a thin layer of stuffing on each fillet and roll up. Poach or steam, in foil, about 10 minutes. Serve decorated with grapes.

Mildred Lathbury in *Excellent Women* saw what others would take to be her role when she heard of Julian Malory's engagement, and she ate appropriately: "After the service I went home and cooked my fish. Cod seemed a suitable dish for a rejected one and I ate it humbly without any kind of sauce or relish." If she had not taken the humbler part, she might have used this recipe.

COD FILLETS WITH CHEESE

2 cod fillets

2 tablespoons butter, softened

1 small onion, grated

¼ cup (30 g) grated cheese

Salt and pepper to taste

Lemon slices for garnish (optional)

Grill the fillets on one side about 4 minutes under a medium grill. Cream the butter, beat in the onion and cheese, and season to taste. Spread butter mixture on uncooked side of fillets and grill an additional 6 minutes. Serve with slices of lemon, if desired.

"I had to put back dinner half an hour, but luckily it was only a fish pie." This from Wilf Bason in *A Glass of Blessings*, who catered so splendidly for his priests at the clergy house. (" 'Bason or Basin—is that his name?' chuckled Sybil. 'That might be a good omen. At least it has a domestic sound about it.' ")

A slightly more ambitious fish pie that shouldn't be kept waiting is this one.

SOUFFLÉ FISH PIE

¾ pound (350 g) white-fleshed fish

2 cups (600 ml) milk

Sprig of fresh fennel

3 tablespoons butter

3 tablespoons flour

¼ pound (110 g) mushrooms

Butter or oil for sautéing

½ cup (150 ml) small peeled shrimps

FOR THE SOUFFLÉ TOPPING

6 tablespoons butter

3 eggs, separated

¼ cup (75 ml) heavy cream

½ cup (60 g) grated cheese

Salt and pepper to taste

Poach fish in milk with fennel, then discard fennel, reserve fish, and use milk to make a white sauce with butter and flour. Slice mushrooms and sauté in butter or oil until tender. Flake fish and place in a greased ovenproof dish, alternating with white sauce, shrimps, and mushrooms.

To make the soufflé topping, melt butter in a double saucepan over hot water, add egg yolks, cream, cheese, and seasonings and cook, stirring, about 6 minutes, or until thickened. Set aside to cool. Preheat oven to 350°F (180°C). Whip egg whites until soft peaks form, then fold into cooled sauce. Pour over fish pie and bake about 12 minutes, until lightly browned and heated through.

To finish this section, we have included an excellent vegetable dish for serving with main courses. *Pommes Anna* was served at the lunch with Philip Larkin in April 1977.

POMMES ANNA

1½ pounds (700 g) potatoes

6 tablespoons butter or margarine

Salt and freshly ground black pepper to taste

Preheat oven to 325°F (160°C). Peel potatoes and slice them thinly. Rinse under cold water to remove excess starch, and dry with a cloth. Grease an ovenproof dish and arrange the potatoes in layers, placing small pieces of butter and seasonings at intervals. Place a piece of buttered paper on top and cover with a lid. Cook in a slow oven for at least 1½ hours, or until potatoes are tender.

Lunch and Supper Dishes

Mildred Lathbury, Emma Howick, and Norman are all making use of eggs for their solitary meals.

I made myself what seemed an extravagant lunch of two scrambled eggs, preceded by the remains of some soup, and followed by cheese, biscuits and an apple.

——EXCELLENT WOMEN

It would have to be an omelette, the kind of thing that every woman is supposed to be able to turn her hand to, but something was wrong with Emma's omelette this evening—the eggs not enough beaten, the tablespoon of water omitted, something not quite as it should be.

——A FEW GREEN LEAVES

"Oh, I just shove everything into the frying-pan," Norman said, as she knew he would—"omelettes and all. Not that you can really call it an omelette, the kind of thing I make."

——QUARTET IN AUTUMN

PIPÉRADE

2 cloves garlic, chopped

1 shallot, minced

5 tablespoons butter

3 green peppers, peeled, seeded, and chopped

¾ pound (350 g) tomatoes, peeled, seeded, and chopped

Salt and pepper to taste

5 eggs

3 tablespoons milk

Sauté garlic and shallot in butter until soft, then add peppers and cook about 5 minutes. Stir in tomatoes, season, and simmer until tender. Beat together eggs and milk, season, and pour over vegetables. Cook until set, turn onto a hot dish, and surround with buttered toast fingers.

Letty, in *Quartet in Autumn* (who made omelettes in her own special omelette pan), was persuaded by Father G., "the efficient bossy clergyman," to choose *Oeufs Florentine* for lunch on the day of Marcia Ivory's funeral "because it sounded attractive":

[Father G.] himself had a steak, Edwin grilled plaice, and Norman cauliflower au gratin. "I don't feel like much," Norman added, subtly making the others feel that they ought not to have felt like much either.

—QUARTET IN AUTUMN

OEUFS FLORENTINE

2 tablespoons butter

2 tablespoons flour

1 cup (300 ml) milk

½ cup (60 g) grated cheese

Cooked spinach, about 8 ounces (225 g)

4 eggs

Make a white sauce with the butter, flour, and milk. Add half the cheese and set aside. Put the hot spinach in an ovenproof dish, poach the eggs, and place them on top. Cover with the sauce, sprinkle with the remaining cheese, and grill until well browned.

Cauliflower cheese, macaroni cheese, shepherd's pie, toad-in-the-hole—these are all names associated with English food and all are enjoyed—or not—by characters in the novels:

"Oh dear, I'm afraid you haven't enjoyed your lunch, Miss Prior," said Belinda, who now felt near to tears. "Don't you like cauliflower cheese?"

"Oh yes, Miss Bede, I do sometimes," said Miss Prior in an offhand tone, not looking up from her work. . . . Then Belinda looked again at the tray, wondering what she could say next. And then, in a flash, she realized what it was. It was almost a relief to know, to see it there, the long, greyish caterpillar.

—SOME TAME GAZELLE

PAIN DE CHOU-FLEUR

¾ pound (350 g) cooked cauliflower

1½ cups (450 ml) thick white sauce

4 eggs, lightly beaten

¾ cup (90 g) grated cheese

Salt and pepper to taste

Pinch of nutmeg

Sieve or purée cauliflower, mix it with white sauce, then add eggs, grated cheese, seasonings, and nutmeg, mixing well to combine. Pour into a greased mold, cover, and simmer in a covered saucepan filled one-third up the side with boiling water, or use a steamer, for 40 minutes.

When Jane "got home she found that Mrs. Glaze had left her a shepherd's pie, a dish she particularly disliked, to put in the oven." *(Jane and Prudence)*

And the same dish must have had bad associations for Edwin in *Quartet in Autumn*: "Edwin had come home one evening some years ago to find his wife Phyllis unconscious in the kitchen, about to put a shepherd's pie in the oven."

But shepherd's pie is a classic dish and can be very good.

SHEPHERD'S PIE

2 onions, chopped

Oil or drippings

1 pound (450 g) minced lamb

1 carrot, finely chopped

Salt and pepper to taste

Mixed herbs to taste

Pinch of cinnamon

1 tablespoon flour

1 cup (300 ml) lamb stock

1 tablespoon tomato purée

Mashed potato

Fry onions in drippings until soft. Add minced lamb and carrot and cook about 10 minutes. Add seasonings, herbs, and cinnamon, then stir in flour and cook 2 to 3 minutes. Stir in stock and tomato purée and simmer gently for about 30 minutes. Preheat oven to 400°F (200°C). Transfer mixture to a shallow ovenproof dish, spread the mashed potato on top, roughing with a fork, and bake 25 minutes, or until heated through and lightly browned.

Moussaka is sometimes described as "Greek shepherd's pie," Emma Howick realized as she turned her anthropologist's eye to considering what might be forthcoming for supper:

What did people in the village eat? she wondered. Sunday evening supper would of course be lighter than the normal weekday meal, with husbands coming back from work. The shepherd's pie, concocted from the remains of the Sunday joint, would turn up as a kind of *moussaka* at the rectory, she felt, given Daphne's passionate interest in Greece. Others would be taking out ready-prepared meals or even joints of meat from their freezers, or would have bought supper dishes at the supermarket with tempting titles and bright attractive pictures on the cover.

—A FEW GREEN LEAVES

But to be correct, *moussaka* must include aubergines.

MOUSSAKA

2 aubergines

Oil for frying

1 pound (450 g) minced lamb or beef

2 onions, sliced

Tin of tomatoes, about 2 cups (600 ml)

1 tablespoon chopped parsley

Pinch of cinnamon

Pinch of nutmeg

Salt and pepper to taste

2 eggs, lightly beaten

1 cup (300 ml) white sauce, cooled (plain yogurt may be substituted)

½ cup (60 g) grated cheese

Slice unpeeled aubergines lengthwise, sprinkle with salt if desired, and set aside to drain. Rinse and dry, then fry in oil until browned, and set aside. In the same pan, lightly fry meat and onions for about 10 minutes, then add tomatoes, parsley, spices, and seasonings, and simmer 20 minutes. Preheat oven to 350°F (180°C). Grease a square baking tin and fill with alternating layers of aubergine slices and meat mixture. For the topping, add eggs to the white sauce and mix well, then stir in grated cheese and pour over casserole. Bake 45 minutes, until the top is browned and the meat mixture firm enough to cut into squares.

"Shall we have *moussaka* or do you like those little meatballs or kebab or something?" . . . Emma was reminded of Daphne, perhaps even now preparing a Greek meal on the outskirts of Birmingham. . . .

—A FEW GREEN LEAVES

Claudia Pettifer was giving Emma lunch in a Greek restaurant. They chose the *moussaka* ("safer," perhaps) but the meatballs are very good and we often made them at home.

KEFTEDHES

½ pound (225 g) finely ground beef

1 onion, chopped

2 slices stale bread

1 tablespoon grated cheese

Pinch of thyme

Pinch of oregano

Salt and pepper to taste

Minced garlic to taste

2 eggs

Flour

Oil for frying

Combine meat and onion in a bowl. Soak bread in water, squeeze out excess, and mash with a fork. Add this, with grated cheese, herbs, seasonings, and garlic to the meat mixture. Add 1 egg to make a firm, smooth paste. In a shallow bowl or dish, beat remaining egg with 1 tablespoon water. Divide meat mixture into balls, dip in beaten egg, roll in flour, and fry in hot fat. Best served with rice and tomato sauce.

Phoebe Sharpe in *The Sweet Dove Died* assumes that the vicar's housekeeper is going out to the shop to get fish fingers for the evening meal. In more leisured times, she might have made fish cakes, even with a touch of curry.

CURRIED FISH CAKES

8 ounces (225 g) cooked fish

2 tablespoons butter, melted

8 ounces (225 g) mashed potato

1 egg, lightly beaten

1 tablespoon chopped parsley

1 dessertspoon curry powder

Flour

Oil or butter for frying

Flake the fish, add melted butter, mashed potato, egg, parsley, and curry powder, and mix well to combine. Mold into flat, round cakes, dust with flour, and sauté in oil or butter until lightly browned on both sides.

"There is a table in the corner," he said. "I know this waitress, and she's kept it for us."

Perhaps this is his life as it really is, I thought, threading my way among the crowded tables; he comes to places like this every day. My first feeling of disappointment now gave way to one of pleasure that he should consider me the kind of person who could fit into his ordinary routine in this way. It seemed to mark an advance in our relationship.

"We could have some beer, if you like," he said, "though you look much too elegant for anything so low."

"I'll have just what you have," I said happily.

"How sweet you are! Would you even have sausage toad if I ordered it?"

"I daresay," I said doubtfully. "I know what it is."

"She knows what it is!" he laughed. "But the roast veal will probably be better."

"You're in a good mood today," I said.

"I hope I always am with you," he said smiling at me.

—A GLASS OF BLESSINGS

Barbara herself ate toad on her first night in the WRNS—July 7, 1943:

For supper we had toad-in-the-hole and bread and jam. After that a talk from First Officer Dixon who was very kind and Third Officer Bolland—Quarters Officer, who was also very nice. A rather restless night, as there was thunder and the mattress and especially pillow are *very* hard.

—A VERY PRIVATE EYE

As she further reports on the twenty-second of that month:

The food is good here, though everything is rather slapdash—there's plenty of it, but we often have to wait for knives.

Barbara and I often made toad.

TOAD-IN-THE-HOLE

⅔ cup (110 g) flour

2 eggs

1 cup (300 ml) milk

½ teaspoon salt

Drippings or bacon fat

½ pound (225 g) sausages

Make a batter with the flour, eggs, milk, and salt. Set aside to rest for a short while. Preheat oven to 425°F (220°C), melt some drippings in a baking tin, add the sausages, and allow them to brown lightly in the oven. Pour batter over sausages, return tin to oven, and continue cooking for about 40 minutes, until batter has risen and set and the sausages are well-browned.

Macaroni cheese was another supper dish of our childhood, but I think Barbara would pass it over in favor of spaghetti, which was again one of the dishes she was good at.

"Tonight," [Adam] was saying, "all I shall be capable of eating is a plate of spaghetti"—he gave it an exaggeratedly Italian pronunciation—"perfectly *al dente*, you understand—exactly twelve and a half minutes, in my opinion—with a sprinkling of Parmesan and a knob of butter."

"Ah, butter," said Tom, seizing on something he had heard of. "What kind of butter?" he was inspired to ask, for he knew that there was a great variety of butters.

"I prefer Danish for spaghetti, otherwise Normandy, of course."

"And what will you drink?" Tom asked, thinking of tea-bag tea, instant coffee or West Oxfordshire water.

"It doesn't matter all that much what one drinks with *spaghetti* so I shall surprise myself. I shall go to my cellar and shut my eyes and reach out to touch a bottle and then, ah then, who knows *what* it might be!"

——A FEW GREEN LEAVES

"At least I can provide you with a reasonable spaghetti," said Penelope, welcoming them at the front door. "And I've got a bottle of Chianti."

"I didn't know you could cook," said Mark.

"Well, I'm learning. It seems the best thing to do now and it gives me an interest." Penelope sounded subdued and looked somehow different. Her hair was smoother and neater and she wore an ostentatiously simple dark blue dress.

"But this is excellent!" exclaimed Mark, in the rather unflatteringly surprised way people sometimes talk when provided with unexpectedly good food.

"And you've put basil in it, like I told you," said Sophia.

"Yes, and I used a *tin* of tomatoes, and cooked it all very slowly for hours and hours."

——AN UNSUITABLE ATTACHMENT

SPAGHETTI BOLOGNESE

1 onion, chopped

Oil or drippings

2 ounces (60 g) finely ground beef

1 ounce (30 g) mushrooms, chopped

½ glass red wine

Small tin of tomatoes, about 1 cup (300 ml)

1 teaspoon chopped basil

Salt and pepper to taste

1 clove garlic, crushed

Spaghetti cooked al dente

Fry onion in oil or drippings until soft but not brown. Add beef and mushrooms and cook about 3 minutes. Pour in wine and let it bubble until reduced by half. Then add tomatoes, basil, seasonings, and garlic. Cover and simmer very slowly for about 1 hour. Serve over spaghetti cooked in plenty of boiling salted water for about 12 minutes.

They were talking in the kitchen, where Catherine had started to prepare a *risotto* with whatever remains she could find. She was mincing some cold meat in her mincing machine, which was called "Beatrice," a strangely gentle and gracious name for the fierce little iron contraption whose strong teeth so ruthlessly pounded up meat and gristle. It always reminded Catherine of an African god with its square head and little short arms, and it was not at all unlike some of the crudely carved images with evil expressions and aggressively pointed breasts which Tom had brought back from Africa.

—LESS THAN ANGELS

I still have Beatrice. I'm sure it was Honor who taught Barbara to make a proper *risotto*, and this is her recipe (*not* using the remains of cold meat).

RISOTTO

4 tablespoons lard or drippings

1 small onion, chopped

2 ounces (60 g) mushroom stalks, chopped

½ pound (225 g) ox or calf's liver, cut in strips

¼ cup (75 ml) tomato sauce

1 clove garlic, crushed with ¼ teaspoon salt

1 cup (225 g) patna or arborio rice

About 1 pint (600 ml) beef stock

½ cup (60 g) grated Parmesan cheese

Heat half the lard or drippings, cook onion until wilted, add mushrooms and liver, and cook over medium-high heat for a few minutes. Remove from heat and stir in tomato sauce, garlic with salt, and rice. Reheat for 1 to 2 minutes, then stir in half the stock and cook gently, stirring, until mixture begins to thicken. Add remaining stock, to just cover mixture, and simmer gently, covered, until rice is tender and stock is absorbed. Remove from heat and scatter half the cheese and the remaining drippings over the rice. Let sit a few minutes to melt, then stir to incorporate. Turn out onto a warmed platter and sprinkle with remaining cheese before serving.

When the party from St. Basil's in *An Unsuitable Attachment* visited Rome, Mervyn Cantrell (he whose packed office lunches might consist of delicacies like an egg-and-bread-crumbed veal cutlet) warned them that they wouldn't like the food:

"Rome—you're welcome to it as far as I'm concerned," said Mervyn spitefully, the day before Ianthe was due to leave with the party from St. Basil's.

"But Rome in the spring, surely that will be lovely," John protested.

"It's not like Paris, you know. I believe it can be uncomfortably hot. And I'm sure you won't like the food. All that canelloni—or all those canelloni, I should say—*very* much overrated."

"Perhaps Ianthe will stick to spaghetti and ravioli," said John, mentioning the better known varieties of pasta which English people would probably be familiar with in tinned form.

"Grated cheese on *everything*," Mervyn went on, "though it is Parmesan, I'll grant you that. Mother would find it much too rich, I know."

"Well, it's a good thing she isn't going, then," said John.

"They tell me you only get that very strong black espresso coffee—not even cappuccino—and the cups are only half full," Mervyn persisted, so that Ianthe had to protest that she wasn't going to Rome only to eat and drink.

—AN UNSUITABLE ATTACHMENT

There is no record that they actually ate *gnocchi alla romana*, but Barbara knew how to make them.

GNOCCHI ALLA ROMANA

1 onion, chopped fine

1 bay leaf

2 cups (600 ml) milk

3 tablespoons semolina or polenta

½ cup (60 g) grated Parmesan cheese

1 tablespoon butter, softened

1 teaspoon prepared Dijon mustard

Salt and pepper to taste

Additional grated cheese for topping

Put onion and bay leaf in milk, bring to a boil, and, when boiling, remove and discard bay leaf. Turn down heat to a simmer, sift in semolina, and stir well. Simmer about 20 minutes, stirring frequently, until thickened. Stir in cheese, butter, mustard, and seasonings. Pour out onto greaseproof paper and spread to ¾-inch thickness. Let cool. When set, cut into squares, lay in a buttered ovenproof dish, sprinkle with additional grated cheese, and brown in a hot oven 400°F (200°C).

Barbara loved Italy, as she records on April 20, 1961:

20 April. To Amalfi and then went to Ravello on the bus. Acres of lemon groves all covered with matting and branches so that you don't see them until you are close to. It is for the lemon groves that one loves Italy—also for oranges with stalks and leaves still on them and the little bundles of dried lemon leaves which you unwrap to reveal a few delicious lemon-flavoured raisins in the middle. The cathedral at Ravello—pulpit supported by lions of marble, walking, their legs going forward. Also in the garden of the Villa Rifolo a little marble lion licking its cub.

—A VERY PRIVATE EYE

In the days before *lasagne* became a universal fast food, Barbara and I used to use a prize-winning newspaper recipe called Venetian Pancakes.

The pancakes don't have to be "thin enough to read a love letter through" (Sybil Forsyth's remark in *A Glass of Blessings*).

VENETIAN PANCAKES

FOR PANCAKE BATTER

2 eggs

1 cup (300 ml) milk

1 cup (180 g) flour, sifted

FOR FILLING

1 small onion, minced

Fat for frying

1½ cups (450 ml) beef stock

1 pound (450 g) finely ground beef

1 clove garlic, minced

2 cups (600 ml) thick cheese sauce

1 cup (110 g) grated Parmesan cheese

Beat together eggs and milk, then add to flour and stir just to combine. Cook on a lightly greased griddle or in a skillet, making 6 or 7 large, thin pancakes. Set aside.

To prepare the filling, fry onion in a little fat, add stock, beef, and garlic and simmer until the liquid is absorbed. Preheat oven to 350°F (180°C). Grease a casserole, put a layer of meat on the bottom, then a pancake, some cheese sauce and Parmesan, and continue layering until all ingredients are used up, ending with a pancake and topping with Parmesan. Cover the casserole and bake 30 to 40 minutes.

Adam Prince, the food inspector, returning from an unusually arduous tour of duty, took up the pint of milk from his doorstep. At least the milkman had got the message this time, though—a shade of displeasure crossed his face—he had not left the Jersey milk, only the "white top," as they called it, which had less cream. Then there were one or two niggling uncertainties in his mind about the restaurants he had just visited and on which he must now write his report. That celery, cleverly disguised in a rich sauce, *had* it come out of a tin? And the mayonnaise with the first course, served in an attractive Portuguese pottery bowl, was it *really* homemade? The fillet of veal, marinaded in Pernod and served with mushrooms, almonds and pineapple in a cream sauce, had been on the rich side and he was now beginning to regret having chosen it. But so often in this work one *had* no choice—it was all in the course of duty. And now what? Too late for coffee, too early for a drink—though when was it ever too early for a glass of Tio Pepe, slightly chilled? And now the rector was approaching, so Adam's thoughts turned to Madeira and possibly a piece of seed cake or a Bath Oliver biscuit. Good plain English food, apart from the drink.

—A FEW GREEN LEAVES

Tinned celery hearts can be used for this recipe, but fresh cooked celery is much nicer.

HAM AND CELERY AU GRATIN

1 large head celery

4 slices cooked ham

1 cup (300 ml) cheese sauce

Bread crumbs

Grated Parmesan cheese

Preheat oven to 350°F (180°C). Simmer the whole celery in salted water until tender. Drain and quarter. Wrap a piece of ham around each portion of celery and place in a greased ovenproof dish. Pour cheese sauce over, sprinkle with bread crumbs and Parmesan, and bake 30 minutes, until browned and heated through. This same recipe may be used for leeks or chicory.

Emma Howick took the bold step of inviting Adam Prince to her small supper party, but "his inclusion meant that the choosing of the menu caused her more anxiety than usual, though she did not know whether he was as critical of food eaten in private houses as of that offered to him in the course of his 'work' " *(A Few Green Leaves)*. The first course, as we know, was a tuna mousse, and it was followed by a French onion tart.

FRENCH ONION TART

Line a flan dish with shortcrust pastry and bake it blind. Fill crust with onions that have been sautéed or boiled until tender and mixed with a thick white sauce (which may be flavored with cheese). Arrange strips of uncooked pastry in a lattice (criss-cross) over the top, or make a lattice of anchovy fillets. Bake in a hot oven (400°F, 200°C) for about 30 minutes.

To have a "light hand with pastry" was, and still is, as Sister Dew pointed out in *An Unsuitable Attachment*, something to be admired. In Ianthe Broome's case, it was her sausage rolls that passed the test.

SAUSAGE ROLLS

1 pound (450 g) sausage meat

8 ounces (225 g) puff, flaky, or shortcrust pastry

1 egg beaten with 1 tablespoon milk

The secret of sausage rolls (apart from the pastry itself) is to roll the sausage meat into long strips and the pastry into strips of matching length, cut to a width of about 4½ inches. Wet one edge of the pastry, put in the long strip of sausage meat, roll up, press lightly, and cut into individual rolls of whatever length you prefer. Preheat oven to 425°F (220°C). Make three V-shaped snips in the top of each roll, and brush with beaten egg. Bake 20 to 25 minutes, until lightly browned and cooked through.

Tea

The things people say:

I never read novels
I never watch television
I never eat jam
I never have tea.

——A VERY PRIVATE EYE

The next day after lunch Flora got out the best tea service and began washing the cups and plates, for it was some time since they had been used. Lovingly she swished the pink-and-gold china in the hot soapy water and dried each piece carefully on a clean cloth. Tea could be laid on the low table by the fire, she decided, with the cloth with the wide lace border. Mrs. Glaze had eventually been persuaded to make a Victoria sandwich cake, there were little cakes from the Spinning Wheel and chocolate biscuits, and Flora intended to cut some cucumber sandwiches and what she thought of as "wafer-thin" bread and butter.

——JANE AND PRUDENCE

Surely an ideal tea, planned by Jane Cleveland's daughter. Barbara was remembering the tea service (and the tablecloth) from teatimes in the past with our grandmother and aunts in Oswestry.

As for making the tea, when her mother asked her to go and put the kettle on, Flora would no doubt have followed the golden rules: warming the teapot with a little boiling water, pouring that away, then putting in one spoonful of tea for each person and "one for the pot" (there might well have been a silver tea-caddy spoon in the family and she wouldn't have heard of tea bags), taking the teapot to the kettle and filling it with the freshly boiled water, covering it with a tea cozy, and allowing it to stand for three or four minutes before pouring it through a strainer into the cups. We are not told whether the tea was Indian or Chinese, or whether slices of lemon were offered as an alternative to milk—she would not have used cream!

Mrs. Glaze would have used this traditional recipe for her cake.

VICTORIA SANDWICH CAKE

12 tablespoons (180 g) butter

1 cup (180 g) castor or superfine sugar

Vanilla essence

3 eggs

1 cup (180 g) self-raising flour

Raspberry jam

Preheat oven to 425°F (220°C). Beat butter and sugar together until light and creamy. Add a few drops of vanilla essence and beat in eggs, 1 at a time. Sift flour, and fold into batter gently. Put the mixture into two 7-inch (18 cm) sandwich tins that have been greased and dusted with flour. Bake 17 to 20 minutes, until done. To sandwich, spread slices with raspberry jam, layer, and sprinkle tops with castor or superfine sugar.

A more challenging cake—though it is in fact easier to make by modern methods—and one on which reputations are made and lost, is usually known simply as a *sponge:*

We dare not *ask* for the grace of humility, but perhaps we don't need to when it is so often thrust upon us, thought Sophia, beating together eggs and sugar for a sponge cake, knowing that her cake would not rise as high as Sister Dew's. When she took it from the oven she was pleased with it, but later, placing it on the trestle table in the hall where refreshments were to be served, she saw that Sister Dew's was higher. "So you've made one of *your* sponges," said the latter in a patronising tone. "It looks quite nice."

—AN UNSUITABLE ATTACHMENT

Mr. Bason, in *A Glass of Blessings,* naturally excelled at it: "Now, Mrs. Forsyth, do try some of my sponge. I think you will find it very light."

I think Barbara did take up the challenge of the sponge, as I remember her making it many times for church bazaars and for home eating, but as there are so many opinions as to method, heat of oven, etc., I shall not risk her reputation by giving a recipe!

At opposite ends of the teatime scale, one might say, are rock buns and fairy cakes:

Emma wished she had won the wine, but she had the quince preserve and a plastic bag containing six rock buns.

—A FEW GREEN LEAVES

Father Anstruther shook his head, then took a plate and wandered off to choose his tea. "Fairies," he murmured, "who was it now who used to make such deliriously light fairies?"

—AN UNSUITABLE ATTACHMENT

ROCK BUNS

1⅓ cups (225 g) flour

Pinch of salt

6 tablespoons (90 g) cold margarine

½ cup (90 g) sugar

1 teaspoon mixed spice

½ cup (90 g) currants and/or sultanas

About 2 tablespoons chopped candied lemon, orange, or mixed peel

1 egg, lightly beaten

Milk to mix

Preheat oven to 425°F (220°C). Sift together the flour and salt, rub in the margarine, then add sugar, spice, fruit, and peel. Mix with egg and milk to form a stiff dough. Arrange on a greased baking sheet in rough heaps, and bake about 20 minutes.

FAIRY CAKES (OR QUEEN CAKES)

8 tablespoons (110 g) butter

⅔ cup (110 g) castor or superfine sugar

2 eggs

1 cup (180 g) flour

½ teaspoon baking powder

Milk, if necessary

Lemon juice, almond flavoring, vanilla essence, or dried fruit to taste

Preheat oven to 425°F (220°C). Cream butter and sugar, then beat in the eggs, 1 at a time. Sift together the flour and baking powder, and add to the butter, adding milk if necessary to make a soft dough. Add the flavoring of your choice, then drop by the teaspoonful into greased small muffin tins or molds and bake 20 minutes.

Attempting to lighten the mood of their tea, Humphrey suggested that Leonora might like a date and walnut slice. She would have refused even if she hadn't lost her appetite, as she preferred something like a marron gâteau, "delicate worms of chestnut purée and cream on the lightest of foundations"—which she found a better cake for trying times *(The Sweet Dove Died)*.

Barbara probably wouldn't have rejected a date and walnut loaf like the one Honor has made.

DATE AND WALNUT LOAF

1 cup (180 g) self-raising flour

1 teaspoon mixed spice

½ teaspoon bicarbonate of soda

2 tablespoons sugar

¾ cup (125 g) chopped dates

¾ cup (125 g) walnut pieces

2 tablespoons (30 g) margarine

1 tablespoon golden or light corn syrup

1 tablespoon malt extract

2 tablespoons milk

Preheat oven to 350°F (180°C). Sift together flour, spice, and bicarbonate of soda. Add sugar, dates, and walnuts. Heat together margarine, syrup, malt, and milk, then pour over dry ingredients and mix well. If the mixture is too stiff, add a little extra milk. Turn into a greased loaf tin and bake about 45 minutes, or until done.

Flora Cleveland had not included scones in that uncomfortable tea for Mr. Oliver, where there had been "too much passing of sandwiches and enquiries about who took sugar." They are very much a part of the English tea menu and were certainly eaten regularly by Belinda and Harriet Bede in *Some Tame Gazelle*. "As she had expected, Harriet was waiting impatiently in the drawing room. The tea was already in, and the hot scones stood in a little covered dish in the fireplace."

Humphrey Boyce in *The Sweet Dove Died*, having regretfully dismissed from his mind a woodland seduction scene, suggested tea, "seeing Leonora's dark beauty against a background of chintz and home-made scones."

Scones needn't always be served hot, but they must be freshly made.

SULTANA SCONES

1⅓ cups (225 g) flour

1 teaspoon cream of tartar

½ teaspoon bicarbonate of soda

4 tablespoons (60 g) cold butter or margarine

2 tablespoons sugar

⅓ cup (60 g) sultanas

About ½ cup (150 ml) milk

Egg or milk wash

Preheat oven to 450°F (230°C). Sift together flour, cream of tartar, and bicarbonate of soda. Rub in the butter, add sugar and sultanas, and add milk gradually to make a soft, nonsticky dough. Roll out onto a floured board to ½-inch thickness, and cut into rounds. Brush with egg or milk wash and bake on a greased baking sheet for 15 minutes. Serve with butter and/or cream and jam.

WHOLEMEAL SCONES

1 cup (180 g) wholemeal flour

⅓ cup (60 g) white flour

1 teaspoon cream of tartar

½ teaspoon bicarbonate of soda

4 tablespoons (60 g) cold butter or margarine

2 tablespoons sugar

About ½ cup (150 ml) milk

Egg or milk wash

Preheat oven to 450°F (230°C). Sift together flours, cream of tartar, and bicarbonate of soda. Rub in the butter, add sugar, and add milk gradually to make a soft, nonsticky dough. Roll out on a floured board to ½-inch thickness, and cut into rounds. Brush with egg or milk wash, and bake on a greased baking sheet for 15 minutes. Serve with butter and/or cream and jam.

"Buns and cakes from Boffin's" were a feature of North Oxford tea parties in *Crampton Hodnet*, so that it is unlikely that it was a homemade fruit cake that Edward Killigrew and Jessie Morrow referred to in the chapter "Edwin and Mother Give a Tea Party."

Mrs. Killigrew paused impressively. "I wonder if you would pass me a piece of sandwich cake, dear? I can't take anything very rich."

"Very wise of you, Charlotte," said Miss Doggett. "If only everyone would follow your example," she added, with a glance at Miss Morrow, who was struggling with a piece of sticky fruit-cake.

"Miss Morrow and I are digging our graves with our teeth," said Edward, helping himself to a piece of the same cake.

—CRAMPTON HODNET

We must go back to Sister Dew for a proper plum cake.

"Will you have a piece of cake? Sister Dew brought me this and it's rather good."

"Not one of her sponges, I see."

"No—she evidently thought a man would like something more substantial like this excellent plum cake."

—AN UNSUITABLE ATTACHMENT

She probably used a well-tried recipe. Here is one.

PLUM CAKE

¾ pound (350 g) butter

1⅓ cups (225 g) sugar

4 eggs

2 cups (350 g) flour

½ teaspoon mixed spice

Pinch of salt

¾ cup (110 g chopped glacéed cherries

¾ cup (110 g) raisins

¾ cup (110 g) sultanas

¾ cup (110 g) chopped almonds

¾ cup (110 g) chopped candied lemon, orange, or mixed peel

Grated rind of 1 lemon and 1 orange

Glass of brandy (optional)

Preheat oven to 300°F (150°C). Cream butter and sugar, then add eggs, 1 at a time, beating well after each addition until mixture is stiff and uniform. Sift the flour with the spice and salt, stir well into creamed mixture, then add the cherries, raisins, sultanas, almonds, mixed peel, and rinds, adding brandy, if desired. Combine thoroughly and bake in a tin lined with greased paper for about 3½ hours. Do not let top burn.

"Old Mrs. Killigrew coming *here*?" Mrs. Cleveland raised her head from her book in sudden agitation.

It was a wet afternoon in July, and she and Anthea were sitting by the fire in the drawing-room.

"Yes, old Mrs. Killigrew," Anthea, who was looking out the window, repeated. "By herself, too."

"But she never goes out," said Mrs. Cleveland in bewilderment, "and it's such a wet day. Is there any cake in the house?" she asked frantically. "I suppose we shall have to offer her tea."

"There may be something," said Anthea. "I'll go and warn Ellen."

"Oh, dear, oh, *dear*, she's so difficult to talk to," wailed Mrs. Cleveland.

—CRAMPTON HODNET

If someone had thought to make a parkin, that is a very good cake for keeping.

PARKIN CAKE

4 tablespoons (60 g) margarine

4 tablespoons treacle or molasses

½ cup (90 g) brown sugar

½ cup (150 ml) milk

1 cup (180 g) flour

1 cup (180 g) rolled oats or coarse oatmeal

1 teaspoon bicarbonate of soda

Preheat oven to 300°F (150°C). Melt margarine and treacle together. Stir in brown sugar until dissolved, add a little of the milk, and set aside to cool. Combine flour and oats, and add to the cooled liquid. Dissolve bicarbonate of soda in remaining milk, then stir into batter. Spread batter in a square or oblong tin lined with grease-proof paper and bake about 1¼ hours.

No tea would be complete without at least one kind of homemade jam. Barbara loved jam making, and it is on record that she was actually making plum jam on the day (September 14, 1977) that James Wright of Macmillan rang to congratulate her on two articles about her in *The Times* and *The Guardian* after the publication of *Quartet in Autumn*. She wrote down her recipe:

PLUM JAM

4¾ pounds (about 2.2 kg) Victoria plums

4½ pounds (about 2 kg) sugar

Wash and stone plums, then set in a large pot with sugar. Stir well and let sit overnight. Boil 35 to 40 minutes. Makes eight 1-pound pots and 4 small pots jam.

. . . Today we see that a huge branch has blown down off the elderberry tree in the back (the branch where we hang one end of the clothes line) so that has to be dealt with. A great deal of jam has been made, strawberry and raspberry—jam-making seems to be associated with the publication of novels.

—LETTER TO PHILIP LARKIN, JULY 27, 1978, A VERY PRIVATE EYE

"Oh, here are my mother and my aunt," said Deirdre, jumping up from her chair.

Two middle-aged ladies in neat summer dresses, coming through french windows on to a lawn and carrying trays of tea-things, is a most pleasing and comforting sight, Catherine thought, envying Deirdre who must see it so often.

—LESS THAN ANGELS

This might almost be a description of the tea ceremony organized by the BBC at our cottage for a television program called "Tea with Miss Pym" in June 1977, when Barbara was interviewed by Lord David Cecil (while trying to stop our cat Minerva from putting her paw in the milk jug). But I end this section with the real-life tea we had with Lord David and Lady Rachel at their home in Dorset in that same summer of Barbara's *annus mirabilis*:

19 May. Tea with Lord David Cecil. A comfortable, agreeable room with green walls and some nice portraits. They are so easy to talk to, the time flew. We had Lapsang tea, brown toast, redcurrant jelly and ginger cake.

—A VERY PRIVATE EYE

Puddings
and Desserts

. . . there was a short silence which was broken by Edwin asking what they would like to eat next, "sweet, pudding or dessert, as the Americans say."

—QUARTET IN AUTUMN

Edwin's own idea of a last course for his midday meal in the office was to devour a jelly baby, preferably a black licorice one, but on this occasion he chose caramel pudding. Now, I don't think Barbara knew how to make this, nor would she have been very interested in finding out. Perhaps she might have said, paraphrasing the words of Viola Dace in *No Fond Return of Love*, that she was "not a great pudding eater at the best of times."

"Of course," said Viola, who had been sitting at the kitchen table reading *Encounter*, "I'm not a great marmalade eater at the best of times."

Not a great marmalade eater . . . Dulcie repeated to herself in a kind of despair. "And when would the best of times for eating marmalade be?" she said aloud.

Viola did not answer.

Another five minutes passed and the marmalade was again tested. It really seemed as if the setting point had been passed now. It would go like a kind of syrup.

"People blame one for dwelling on trivialities," said Dulcie, "but life is made up of them. And if we've had one great sorrow or one great love, then who shall blame us if we only want the trivial things?"

She might have made an exception in the case of cheesecake, because Hazel Holt has this recipe, which has been adapted from one found written in Barbara's own hand.

CHEESECAKE

8 ounces (225 g) cream cheese, softened

12 tablespoons (180 g) butter, softened

2 tablespoons ground almonds

½ glass raisin wine (we didn't add this)

1 or 2 wholemeal biscuits, grated

2 eggs

1 cup (300 ml) heavy cream

Currants (if liked)

Pinch of cinnamon powder

Vanilla essence to taste

Sugar to taste (if liked)

Preheat oven to 350°F (180°C). Mix all ingredients and beat well until light. Pour into 2 greased 7-inch sandwich tins and bake 45 minutes. Let cool to set before serving.

In the kitchen Miss Lord was sitting at the table, polishing some little glass dishes.

"Dainty, aren't they," she said. "Just the thing for the sweet. That orange mousse will look lovely in them. Oh, Miss Dace, your shawl! It must've dipped in the soup. Give it to me and I'll wash the fringe."

——NO FOND RETURN OF LOVE

ORANGE MOUSSE

4 eggs, separated

½ cup (90 g) sugar

2 oranges (juice and grated rind)

½ oz (15 g) gelatin

Beat egg yolks with sugar until light and foamy. Add orange juice and heat mixture in the top of a double saucepan, stirring constantly, until thickened. Dissolve gelatin in ½ teacup boiling water to which grated orange peel has been added. Stir this into the egg yolk mixture and set aside to cool. Beat egg whites until stiff, and fold into cooled egg yolk mixture. Pour into a serving dish or individual dishes, cover, and chill before serving.

"I think we need custard powder," said Keith.

"*Custard powder?*" exclaimed Piers in horror. "Good God, whatever do we want custard powder for?"

"To make custard," said Keith flatly.

"You mean *you* want to make custard with it. Well, all right then, as long as you don't expect *me* to eat it."

"He'll eat anything, really," said Keith to me in a confidential tone, gathering his purchases together into a canvas bag not unlike Mr. Bason's. "I always think custard is nice with stewed fruit, don't you, Mrs. Forsyth?"

—A GLASS OF BLESSINGS

POIRES RELIGIEUSES

2 pounds (900 g) pears

4 tablespoons simple syrup

1 package custard mix (to make 1 pint)

1 cup (300 ml) milk

2 tablespoons sugar

4 tablespoons chocolate or cocoa powder

Peel, core, and halve the pears, and stew them in water to cover that has been mixed with the simple syrup. Meanwhile, mix custard mix with milk, sugar, and chocolate powder and prepare as usual (remember, you're only using half the amount of milk called for on the package, so custard will be quite thick). Thin custard with some of the pear juice. To serve, put the pears in a dish and coat them with the sauce. They can be hot or cold.

"One never *quite* knows what wine to drink with gooseberries," said Rodney, turning to James Cash rather apologetically. "I suppose something a little drier than might be considered usual with the sweet—is that about the best one can do?"

I let out a snort of laughter before I realized that Rodney's manner was serious, almost deferential, and that the question was being gravely considered. So James was one of those boring wine men, I thought.

"I think you've hit upon an admirable compromise here," he said politely, "though I believe you could almost get away with one of those outrageously sweet wines—perhaps even a Samos—the kind of thing that seems otherwise to have no possible raison d'être. Perhaps that *is* their raison d'être—to be drunk with gooseberries or rhubarb! If you like I will raise the matter with my own wine merchant—a man of considerable courage, even panache."

"Thank you," said Rodney seriously. "We—my wife and mother, rather—are very fond of gooseberries. We often eat them in one form or another."

"Perhaps they are more a woman's fruit," said Sybil, "like rhubarb. Women are prepared to take trouble with sour and difficult things, whereas men would hardly think it worth while."

—A GLASS OF BLESSINGS

GOOSEBERRY PIE

2 pounds (900 g) gooseberries

Sugar to taste

8 ounces (225 g) shortcrust pastry

Preheat oven to 425°F (220°C). Wash, top, and tail the gooseberries, and put them in a deep pie dish. Sprinkle with sugar according to the desired amount of sweetness. Roll out shortcrust pastry and place over gooseberries. Bake for 40 minutes. Serve with custard or cream.

"Tried Favourites"

This section takes its title from a cookery book that must have been in many homes in the early years of the century. I think it was Scottish in origin, because it described porridge, for instance, as "a capital dish for the bairns." It was by turns practical and didactic.

"I seem to remember a recipe in *Tried Favourites*—a sort of substitute for whisky," said Belinda. "I dare say it would be quite easy to make."

"I think our guests would hardly thank us if we offered them that," said Harriet.

—SOME TAME GAZELLE

The recipes given here were not necessarily in that book, but I am including them for the simple reason that they *were* favorites and appeared regularly in our family.

When one is tired one gets strange fancies. On one occasion when we had the evacuees I fancied I smelled rabbit cooking in church and the altar looked like some celestial Aga.

—A VERY PRIVATE EYE

RABBIT WITH FORCEMEAT BALLS

This is made with a sixpenny or ninepenny rabbit from Oswestry market.

1 rabbit, cut in pieces

Flour seasoned with salt and pepper

Oil or drippings

1 onion, sliced

Sprig of thyme

FOR THE FORCEMEAT BALLS

⅓ cup (60 g) bread crumbs

1 ounce (30 g) shredded suet

2 teaspoons chopped parsley

2 teaspoons chopped thyme

Juice and grated rind of 1 lemon

1 egg

Oil or drippings

Preheat oven to 350°F (180°C). Coat the joints of the rabbit with seasoned flour and brown in oil or drippings in a frying pan. Add onion and cook until soft. Transfer to a casserole and add a sprig of thyme. To remaining fat in frying pan, add an equal amount of seasoned flour and cook, stirring, 2 to 3 minutes. Add 2 cups water and bring to a boil. Pour over rabbit in casserole, cover, and bake about 2 hours.

To prepare the forcemeat balls, mix all ingredients together and form into balls. Fry until browned in oil or drippings, and add to the casserole just before serving. Serve with redcurrant jelly alongside.

IRISH STEW

2 pounds (900 g) neck of mutton (or lamb)

2 pounds (900 g) potatoes

2 carrots

2 onions

A handful of pearl barley

Salt and pepper to taste

Cut the meat into chops and trim off fat. Cut potatoes in quarters, slice carrots and onions, then put all ingredients into a large covered pan. Add 2 cups (600 ml) water and simmer gently, covered, for about 2½ hours.

KEDGEREE

4 tablespoons (60 g) butter

¼ pound (110 g) cooked rice

¾ pound (350 g) cooked haddock, flaked

Salt and pepper to taste

1 egg, lightly beaten

Milk (optional)

1 teaspoon curry powder

Lemon juice to taste

1 hard-boiled egg, chopped

Chopped parsley for garnish

Preheat oven to 300°F (150°C). Melt butter in a frying pan, add cooked rice, fish, seasonings, and beaten egg. Add milk if mixture seems too dry. Then stir in curry powder, lemon juice, and hard-boiled egg. Transfer to an ovenproof dish and bake 25 minutes. Serve garnished with parsley.

STEAMED APPLE PUDDING

"Bertie Booth's Hat" was named after a cousin of our mother.

1⅓ cups (225 g) self-raising flour

Pinch of salt

4 ounces (110 g) shredded suet

1 pound (450 g) cooking apples, peeled, cored, and sliced

Pinch of ground cloves

⅓ to ⅔ cup (60 to 110 g) sugar

Sift flour and salt into a bowl, add the suet, and mix to a firm dough with cold water, adding 1 tablespoon water at a time until dough reaches the right consistency. Grease a 4-cup (1-liter) pudding basin or heatproof bowl. Fit three-quarters of the dough into the basin and mold around the sides, drawing it well up to the top. Fill with apples, cloves, and sugar, and add about 4 tablespoons water. Pat the remaining piece of dough into a round the size of the top of the pudding. Moisten the edges and put it on, pinching the edges together to make a firm seal. Cover with foil and steam 1½ to 2 hours. Turn out and serve with custard.

RAILWAY PUDDING

I don't know how it got this name,
but I suspect it was a joke having to do with raspberry jam.

½ cup (90 g) flour

1 teaspoon bicarbonate of soda

⅓ cup (60 g) sugar

1 teaspoon ground ginger

2 to 3 ounces shredded suet

½ cup (90 g) fresh bread crumbs

1 egg, lightly beaten

¼ cup (75 ml) milk

2 tablespoons raspberry jam

Sift together flour, bicarbonate of soda, sugar, and ginger. Add suet and bread crumbs. Mix in the egg and milk, and stir to a soft consistency. Put the jam in the bottom of a greased pudding basin, pour batter over, cover with foil, and steam for 1½ hours.

TRIFLE

3 small sponge cakes

Strawberry jam

6 macaroons, or 1 ounce (30 g) ratafia biscuits

½ cup (150 ml) sherry

1 ounce (30 g) blanched almonds

1 cup (300 ml) prepared custard, at room temperature

½ cup (150 ml) double or heavy cream

Glacéed cherries and candied angelica for garnish

Split sponge cakes and spread with jam. Put in a dish with macaroons or ratafias and pour sherry over all. Scatter almonds on top, and pour custard over. Whip cream to soft peaks, and spoon over all. Decorate with cherries and angelica.

QUEEN OF PUDDINGS

This is Irena Pym's recipe.

Take 3 parts of a pint of bread crumbs, 1 pint of milk, the rinds of 2 lemons grated, 3 eggs separated, 1 ounce of butter, sugar to taste, and a little raspberry jam. To make pudding, put the bread crumbs into a pie dish with the grated peel and sugar. Bring milk to a boil and stir in butter until melted, then pour over bread crumbs, stirring. Add well-beaten egg yolks and stir to combine. Bake for about 20 minutes in a moderate oven, 350°F (180°C). When done, spread top with jam, then cover with egg whites beaten until stiff with a little castor or superfine sugar. Place again in the oven for a short time to set and brown top.

I sat down at the table without any very high hopes, for both Julian and Winifred, as is often the way with good, unworldly people, hardly noticed what they ate or drank, so that a meal with them was a doubtful pleasure. Mrs. Jubb, who might have been quite a good cook with any encouragement, must have lost heart long ago. Tonight she set before us a pale macaroni cheese and a dish of boiled potatoes, and I noticed a blancmange or "shape," also of an indeterminate colour, in a glass dish on the sideboard.

—EXCELLENT WOMEN

BLANCMANGE

"An Improved Blancmange" was adapted from M. J. Thomas, 1888. It is our grandmother's recipe. She was cooking for at least ten.

Add 4 tablespoons of arrowroot to a pint of cold milk and set aside. Bring to a boil a quart of milk with 2 tablespoons of butter and sugar to taste. Beat up 4 eggs well and add them to the cold milk, then stir into the milk on the fire and bring all to a boil, stirring well until thick and no lumps remain. Pour into a wetted mold and chill till set. Half this quantity would be sufficient to make one dish.

BAKED CUSTARD PUDDING

This was adapted from M. J. Thomas, 1888.

3 cups (900 ml) milk

¼ pound (117 g) sugar

Grated rind of ¼ lemon

4 eggs

Baked shortcrust pastry shell

Freshly grated nutmeg to taste

Heat milk in a saucepan with sugar and lemon rind, then set aside to infuse for 30 minutes, or until the milk is well-flavored. Whisk the eggs until frothy, then add the milk, stirring all the time. Strain into baked shortcrust shell, grate a little nutmeg over the top, and bake in a very slow (about 275°F, 140°C) oven for 30 minutes or longer, until set. The flavor of this pudding may be varied by substituting bitter almonds for the lemon rind, and it may be very much enriched by using half cream and half milk and doubling the quantity of the eggs.

THE "GERTRUDE" CAKE

This was adapted from Irena Pym's recipe. I don't know who Gertrude was.

Take 2 eggs, their weight in butter, sugar, and flour, the juice and grated rind of 1 orange, a tablespoonful of milk, a pinch of baking powder, and icing sugar. To make cake, cream the butter and sugar, add the 2 eggs, well beaten, stir in the milk and orange rind, then add flour and baking powder. Put the batter in a greased tin and spread evenly. Place in a good oven (about 350°F, 180°C) and bake for half an hour, or until done. For the icing, squeeze the juice of the orange into a bowl and add as much icing sugar as necessary to make the right spreading consistency. Put icing on when cake is cooled.

Belinda was silent, wondering if by any chance there were any plums left and whether she would have the courage to bring the Archdeacon a pot of the blackberry jelly which she herself had made a week or two ago. Perhaps when Agatha went away . . . a cake, too, perhaps with coffee icing and filling and chopped nuts on the top, or a really rich fruit cake. . . .

—SOME TAME GAZELLE

This was very popular during our boarding school years.

MOCHA CAKE

8 tablespoons (110 g) butter

⅔ cup (110 g) castor or superfine sugar

2 eggs

⅔ cup (110 g) flour

¼ teaspoon baking powder

1 teaspoon coffee flavoring

Butter icing

Coffee icing

1 ounce (30 g) blanched almonds, toasted and chopped

Cream together butter and sugar, then add eggs, 1 at a time, beating well after each addition. Sift together flour and baking powder, and add to butter mixture. Add coffee flavoring and combine well. Preheat oven to 325°F (170°C). Butter a cake tin, dust with flour, pour in batter, and spread evenly. Bake 1¼ hours. When cooled completely, sandwich with butter icing and top with coffee icing. Decorate with toasted almonds.

SUMMER PUDDING

1½ pounds (700 g) raspberries

½ pound (225 g) redcurrants

½ pound (225 g) sugar

White bread slices, crusts trimmed (enough to line bowl and cover fruit)

Whipped cream

Simmer fruit and sugar slowly over low heat to soften and release juices. Line a bowl, bottom and sides, with bread slices, making sure there is no space between them. Add the fruit to the bowl, reserving some of the juice. Cover the fruit with a complete layer of bread. Put on top a plate that fits inside the bowl and on the plate put a 2- or 3-pound weight. Refrigerate overnight. To serve, remove weight and plate from top, gently run a knife around the edges to loosen pudding, then turn it out onto a large dish, and pour over it the reserved juice. Serve with whipped cream.

TREACLE TART

Shortcrust pastry

5 tablespoons golden syrup, or 1 tablespoon dark corn syrup and 4 tablespoons light corn syrup

⅓ cup (60 g) bread crumbs

Whipped cream

Preheat oven to 375°F (190°C). Line a flan tin with the pastry. Warm the syrup and mix in some of the bread crumbs. Sprinkle remaining bread crumbs over pastry, pour in the syrup mixture, and bake 30 minutes, or until pastry is lightly browned. Serve warm with whipped cream.

BAKED APPLES WITH MINCEMEAT

Large, firm cooking apples

Jar of mincemeat

Whipped cream or brandy butter

Preheat oven to 350°F (180°C). Core apples and score skin with a knife around the middle. Stuff apples with mincemeat and bake in a tin with a little water for about 45 minutes. Serve with whipped cream, brandy butter, or both.

"A FAVOURITE NURSERY DELIGHT"

Honor also remembers making for Barbara "a bowl of groats, fragrant as a corn-field and intriguingly surfaced with little pock marks. Barbara, for some reason, was 'off her food' and couldn't fancy anything till I spoke the magic word 'groats.' To children of pre-war generations, this bedtime cereal was a treat when one was feeling poorly, a symbol somehow of a mother's loving care."

"Groats are the hulled and roasted grains of buckwheat. Barbara's mother, it seemed, had prepared it the hard way. 'Put in cloth with salt and cold water' says the handwritten recipe in Mrs. Pym's cookery book, 'and boil about an hour.' Apparently, she would serve them as an accompaniment to rich meat like goose or duck.

"I had an easier method. I bought a tin of Patent Groats, in powder form, and made them up according to the instructions on the label. 'Mix one or two table-spoons of groats to a paste with a little milk. Add boiling water and simmer till the consistency of thick cream.' Exact quantities forgotten and cannot be checked as, alas, Patent Groats have virtually disappeared from England's nurseries. A sad national loss.

"But it is still sometimes possible to buy packets of the whole grain. These must be very finely ground to a powder (about three times with electric equipment) till no gritty husk remains. This can now be prepared in the same way as Patent Groats. Always stir in the water very slowly. The exact consistency depends on the taste of the eater. I like it as thick as porridge. Serve hot with milk and demerara sugar or, better still, with cream and brown sugar. But what has happened to the pock marks these days? No sign. Another dream of childhood vanished. . . ."

Permission for excerpts from the novels *An Academic Question, An Unsuitable Attachment, Crampton Hodnet, Excellent Women, A Few Green Leaves, A Glass of Blessings, Jane and Prudence, Less Than Angels, No Fond Return of Love, Quartet in Autumn, Some Tame Gazelle,* and *The Sweet Dove Died* by Barbara Pym, and *A Very Private Eye: An Autobiography in Diaries and Letters,* edited by Hazel Holt and Hilary Pym, has been granted by E. P. Dutton, a division of NAL Penguin Inc.

copyright © 1981 The Estate of Barbara Pym

cover design by Mimi Bark

ISBN 978-1-4804-0805-0

This edition published in 2013 by Open Road Integrated Media
180 Varick Street
New York, NY 10014
www.openroadmedia.com

BARBARA PYM EBOOKS

FROM OPEN ROAD MEDIA

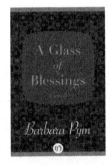
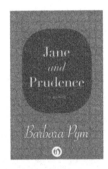

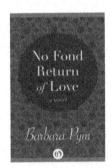

Available wherever ebooks are sold

OPEN ROAD
INTEGRATED MEDIA

Open Road Integrated Media is a digital publisher and multimedia content company. Open Road creates connections between authors and their audiences by marketing its ebooks through a new proprietary online platform, which uses premium video content and social media.

CPSIA information can be obtained
at www.ICGtesting.com
Printed in the USA
BVOW04s1644160817
492254BV00017B/709/P

9 781480 408050